AF489265

What is Gerrymandering?

for kids

Written by Jeffrey Lane

That's a big word! 🤯

Gerry-man-der-ing - What a big word! Let's dive right in! Gerrymandering describes people can vote based on where they live.

In order to understand gerrymandering, there are two words we need to understand first: **sort** and **vote**.

Let's begin with **sort!**

Let's sort!

Have you ever decided to sort a group of things based on its shape, color or use? Colorful beads, puzzle pieces or building blocks can all be sorted based on their shape, color or even what people they they are used. **Sorting means to organize objects together**.

🎉 You know how to sort!

Great job understanding sorting. Now learn what it means to vote!

Let's vote! 🙋

Imagine you were in your class at school and the teacher said, "We have two special treats to choose from today!"

"Together, we will decide on which treat to eat."

Cookies  or ice cream 🍦 ?

"The first choice is cookies and the second is vanilla ice cream."

Which one would you choose?

pone
Yogurt
Pesca

Who wants cookies?

"Please raise your hand if you think we should have cookies today," the teacher asks.

Two children raise their hands.

Who wants ice cream?

Then the teacher asks, "now please raise your hand if you think we should have vanilla ice cream today"

And 10 children raise their hands!

Ice cream wins!

Voting is choosing one option instead of a different option. Because more children (10) voted for ice cream than those who voted for cookies (2), the class chose ice cream!

🎉 You know how to vote!

Great job understanding voting. Now let's talk about the big word - gerry-man-der-ing!

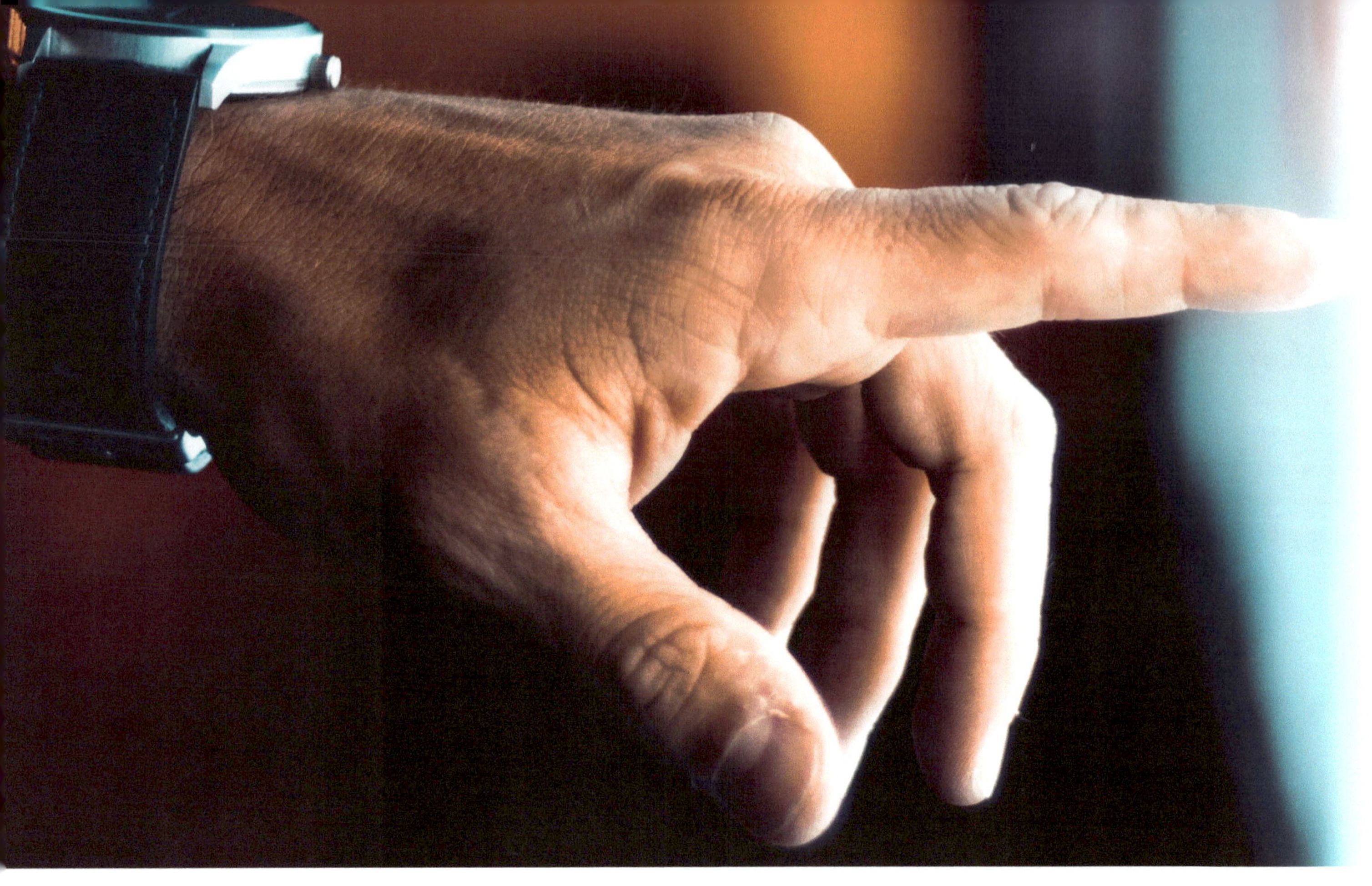

Now if a teacher decided they wanted to only eat cookies and then decided to move *all* the kids out of your class who voted for ice cream - this would be called ***gerrymandering***.

Gerrymandering means controlling the vote by choosing the people who can vote.

What about ice cream?

Because the teacher wanted cookies and decided who could vote, the children who wanted ice cream would not get ice cream today 🙁.

What if I wanted cookies?

Have you ever decided to sort a group of things based on its shape, color or use? Colorful beads, puzzle pieces or building blocks can all be sorted based on their shape, color or even what people they they are used.

Sorting means to organize objects together.

What happened to my vote?

Votes are important because they represent what you, the individual want.

Gerrymandering can cancel out your vote and instead group people based an outside interest.

If you'd like your vote to be counted in the future, you have to let people know. Cconsider writing a letter to your congress person and letting them know today!

To write your representative, please have your adult visit:
https://www.house.gov/htbin/findrep

Thanks for reading!